Own Your Money: The Financial Foundation

Building Financial Confidence Series, Volume 1

SHIRLEY STEPHENS

Published by SHIRLEY STEPHENS, 2025.

OWN YOUR MONEY: THE FINANCIAL FOUNDATION

First edition. December 1, 2025.

ISBN: 979-8232268923

Written by SHIRLEY STEPHENS.

Also by SHIRLEY STEPHENS

Building Financial Confidence Series
Own Your Money: The Financial Foundation

The Awakening Series
Please Don't Eat the Script: Waking Up from the Silent Performance

Standalone
Before You Sign Anything
Built on Reputation
The Power Seat
The Blue Print & The Breakdown
The War Manual: Tactical Prayer Strategies For Women

Table of Contents

Preface

Own Your Money: The Financial Foundation, *Building Financial Confidence. (Build Wealth. Live Free. Leave Legacy.)*

Why You Need This Series

I was talking to a friend a few months ago about everything, and yet nothing specific. She said that she had a financial adviser, and her mother did too; the financial adviser's job was to show them how to use their money efficiently and effectively. While she was speaking, I spaced off a bit, not disinterested, but pondering.

I started to imagine how much steadier that conversation would sound for so many Americans, namely, one out of every eight, who rely on SNAP benefits to feed their families. A financial advisor might not even be in the conversation for them. The real question is not "Who should I invest with?" It's "How do I even begin?"

This idea lingered with me long after the conversation ended, sparking a deeper reflection. That's ultimately why I chose to go all in twice first on this book and then its sequel series.

This is not only a guide to dollars and cents but also one of freedom and foundation. It's about walking through the steps of making your money work for you and then figuring out how to teach that same money to work for others.

Because when your money goes from being a millstone around your neck to being your tool, everything changes. You think differently. You plan differently. You live differently.

As you work through this first book, prepare to embark on a journey built upon small, deliberate steps. Each installment in this series is intentionally designed to be manageable. This matters because genuine transformation occurs in small segments. A journey is, in reality, a series of destinations, each one showing you how to build confidence, clarity, and consistency with your finances.

I didn't have a financial mentor when I was young to teach me how to manage money. There was no manual that nobody sat us down to show us how to make it, keep it, and grow it.

I was brought up to get by, work hard, and pay the bills. And that mentality kept us afloat, it sustained our families, but it didn't teach us how to thrive, to go about the business of creating wealth, or to build a legacy that outlives us.

I had to learn the long way.

I learned to manage enough to get by: how to budget, stretch, and make it work. But what no one ever taught me is how to partner with money, how to view it not as a source of stress and shame, but rather as a living tool. A tool for freedom. A tool for influence. A tool for change.

And this series is my giving you what I wish somebody had given me: a foundation. A script to rewrite the one we were handed about money, and that starts not with scarcity but with training.

You'll see as you read that this isn't just about numbers or balance sheets. It's about mindset. It's about stewardship. And it's about learning how to move from 'getting by' to getting ahead, and from getting ahead.

Because true financial freedom isn't just what you make, it's what you know. And once you grasp it, you will never look at money the same way again.

Money isn't about buying things; it's about creating options. It's being in a place where, if someone you love truly needs something that requires real help, you are in a position to step right in and do so without shame, guilt, or lack. It's about access, and access is priceless. Money is a tool. Others have always had it. The aim of this book is to put that same access directly into your hands and prepare a path for women to build wealth that isn't limited to paying bills but also ignites real change.

How to Use This Book

You may know how to budget, but do you know how to do it effectively? There's a difference between forcing numbers on paper to line up and designing a system that generates wealth in real life. This book can help you look straight at what you're doing financially now.

As you make your way through the chapters, this is all that you have to do:

• Revise what isn't working.

• Go back and see the stuff you've been avoiding.

• Change routines and systems you're stuck in.

• Recognize where you're already on the right course and keep going. Consider this book a mirror and a mentor. It's not here to judge you; it's here to challenge you. Each tool, each story, each strategy is created to meet you where you are and point you in the direction of where you long to be.

Here, you'll discover how to:

- Learn the fundamentals of budgeting, saving, and credit without being overwhelmed.

- Get your money growing with straightforward, practical steps for anyone.

- End the cycle of survival and create systems that serve you.

- Think of money in terms of impact, not simply income.

- Leave the next generation both a legacy of material and of wisdom.

Why read this? Because your money story doesn't have to end where it began. Why share this? Since every woman you know, your sister, daughter, or friend, should know that money's not only about getting more; it's about becoming a woman who can do more, give more, and change more.

This is not just another financial book. Use it as your permission slip to act now: stop surviving and start thriving, creating your lasting financial imprint today.

Table of Contents

Part V: From Surviving to Stable

When you get punched in the gut

As a teenager, I was quietly educated about personal finance in small but powerful ways. I was already running my own summer babysitter's club at the tender age of thirteen. I got a part-time job the following year, and by the time I was sixteen, I had two part-time jobs, working to save money and pay cash for my first car. That was the plan. Unfortunately, as life often does, things didn't unfold quite the way I hoped. Fast forward some years, and married with two kids, working full time (maybe more than that; who can keep track?), and navigating the intricacies of managing money as a team. I discovered that marriage creates a dual responsibility for managing money. Spending any denomination of money frequently calls for a compromise, conversation, or even concession.

Meanwhile, in my professional life, I was responsible for millions of dollars in the corporate world. However, what I witnessed time and again in both families and businesses was how women, especially, are often required to walk a fine line between submission and self-sufficiency. We learn to juggle, and shift, and compromise. And all too often, when the marriage or partnership falls apart, we're prisoners of needing to start not only from a place of confidence but also from our own financial cushion.

I've seen companies fall apart due to poor financial management, and I've seen women with immense potential wonder whether they can maximize their potential. How to grow it, how to multiply it, how to continue giving generously even when life has taken more than its fair share. And that's how we got to this book, this conversation, this moment. I'm sharing what I wish I knew differently, the lessons that defined me, and a few that broke me just enough to come back smarter.

My first tough lesson went like this: after we sold our first house, we came away with $35,000 in our hands, and upon my parents' urging, we went to find a financial adviser. It felt like the right thing to do; it was safe and responsible, grown-up. We didn't receive any information about how our money was being invested.

No word, no news, nothing to let us know how the funds were being managed. When I finally reached out to the brokerage firm to withdraw whatever was remaining, I got the callback nobody ever wants: the account was zero, and I owed fees to the brokerage. The shock was more than I could bear. The loss was not only financial but emotional. I had trusted a man with my family's future, and I hadn't even known enough to ask the right questions.

That day, I made a vow to myself. I will never again relinquish my financial power without knowing how my money is being managed. That was the big lesson for me. There were plenty more to come. But if telling my story can prevent just one person from making the same mistake, every dollar I lost and tear that has fallen will have been worth it.

Introduction: The Dealership Story, Why We Need a Financial Foundation

A couple of years ago, Mary went to purchase a car from a General Motors dealership. And the first thing Mary did was park her old car smack in the middle of the lot and leave it. Mary was an intentional buyer; she wanted a top-of-the-line luxury SUV. She determined that her credit was bad without ever checking it.

Mary knew she wanted the luxury utility vehicle, and now that she was here, she had to get it. The salesperson didn't have the model she wanted, but he assured her they could find one from another General Motors dealership for her. Two weeks later, she came back for the "big reveal." She was presented with a big black Chevrolet Suburban jammed with amenities, rather than her dream car. The sales price was not negotiated by Mary.

Checking her credit before heading to the car dealership was not part of the research process. When it was time to pay for her new vehicle, she was ushered off to the finance department and was informed that her credit "wasn't that good." It was her worst fear come true. In Mary's mind, she was correct and signed up for an 84-month contract at a high interest rate.

The painful truth: Mary's credit was, in fact, good. She might qualify for better terms and lower pricing. But because she did not understand the rules of the game, she left thousands of dollars on the table.

The Moral of the story: She wasn't being careless or irresponsible. She simply hadn't been taught how to plan for financial freedom. That woman could be me, you, or anyone. We do the work, we show up, and we take care of others, but when it comes to money, for many of us, there's an absence of true knowledge and a reliance on scraps of advice, myths, or fear.

This book changes that.

Here, you'll learn how to:

• Read your paycheck like a pro.

• Be the master of your checking account, and make it your command center.

• Save 'big' for big purchases, but avoid debt traps.

• Learn all about credit and how you can make the most of it.

• Establish a base that's going to keep getting stronger. We'll use stories, numbers, scripture, and real-life illustrations. Yes, we'll even discuss coffee runs, meals out, and a meal plan because financial empowerment is not only about Wall Street. It's about your groceries, your gas tank, and how you spend today.

Proverbs 31:16 "She considers a field, and buys it: with the fruit of her hands she plants a vineyard." That's an image of a woman who values herself, knows how to manage her money, and is investing it in what will bring her happiness in the future.

That woman can be you.

Welcome to the foundation.

It's time to quit surviving and start prospering.

Chapter 2
The Credit Game

The Real Talk

Credit is one of the least understood aspects of personal finance. For others, it seems like freedom. For some, that feels like a draw. Women, in particular, have been warned: "Don't leave yourself with the burden of debt."

"Credit cards are dangerous." "Only men know how to play the system." The truth is this: credit isn't good or bad. It's a tool. It can be like fire. It has the ability to warm your home but also burn it down. Men have been schooled on how to play this credit game; women all too often have been told not to touch it.

This chapter flips that script.

Foundation Reminder:

Credit is not a matter of fear. It's about strategy.

What Credit Really Is

Credit is, at its core, simple: it's borrowed trust. A lender is telling you, "We trust you enough to give you money today, but we know that tomorrow you're going to pay us back."

• These credit card loans, car loans, and mortgages are all simply borrowed money with a promise to pay back.

• If you honor the promise → trust builds up (credit score goes up).

• Break the promise → pay more (interest, late fees, and a lower score).

Imagine credit as a personal reputation. Protect it, and doors open. Ignore it, and doors slam.

How the Credit Trap Works

For example, say you charge a $1,000 purchase on a credit card at 20 percent interest and pay only the minimum each month.

• It might take more than five years to pay it back.

• You'll give the bank nearly $600 more in interest.

Translation: If you don't pay in full, you're working for the credit card company, not the other way around.

Buy Now, Pay Later(BNPL)

Numbers First Firms like Klarna, Afterpay, and Affirm offer to make it easier on your wallet by dividing a purchase into bite-sized payments.

• Example: Purchase $200 = $50 today, then pay $50 every two weeks until fully paid off.

• If you make a late payment, → late fees ($7–$15).

• Some plans charge interest (10%-30%) on long-term options.

• Multiple purchases stack. $200 shoes, plus $600 of furniture, plus a $100 makeup haul → suddenly you owe $225 every two weeks across multiple apps.

BNPL(buy now, pay later) feels so painless; yet this is just debt dressed up as installments.

The trick not everyone knows:

The Closing Date

Paying by the due date is what most borrowers believe is good enough: That means paying on time. Wrong.

The closing date is the day your balance is reported to credit bureaus.

• For example: Closing Date = 15th. Due date = 10th of the following month.

• You clear your card by the 14th of the month → they report a $0 balance.

• That ramps up your score, though you used a card.

Smart move: Pay by the closing date, not just the due date.

Debit vs. Credit: Understand the Difference

• Debit Card: Cash gets yanked immediately out of your checking account. No debt, but also less fraud protection.

• Credit Card: Money borrowed. Robust fraud coverage, rewards, and perks, but dangerous if you don't pay in full.

Foundation Tip:

Treat credit like a debit card. Spend only what you have already budgeted for.

How to Master Your Checking Account

It's Your Command Post

Your checking account is where the game of credit truly begins.

If you're not sure what is coming in and going out, you'll always feel behind.

Types of Checking Accounts:

- Basic (standard, sometimes fees).
- Free/Online (no fees, app-based).
- Rewards (cash back or points).
- Interest-bearing (small % earned).
- Student/Teen (simplified, low fees).

Why It Matters:

- Safety: It's FDIC insured up to $250,000 (and cash under the mattress has a value of zero).
- Access: Debit cards, direct deposits, and bill pay.
- Keeping track: Statements reveal precisely where money is going.
- Tools: Lots of accounts round up purchases to help you auto-save.

Building Foundation Trick: Use your checking accounts as a command center, moving that money to bills, savings, and investments with precision.

Safeguard Yourself: Credit Reports and Monitoring

- Get Your Free Report: AnnualCreditReport.com (3 bureaus, annual).
- Set Up Monitoring: Free tools can be useful to monitor your credit, like Credit Karma or Experian.
- Freeze if Necessary: Guards against fraudsters opening accounts in your name.

Lesson: You wouldn't dismiss your health checkups. Don't ignore your credit checkups.

The Biblical Anchor ⟐ Proverbs 22:7: "The borrower is servant to the lender." Debt is not bad, but it does lead to bondage. We don't want to avoid using credit entirely; we want to become so proficient with it that we maintain the upper hand, rather than being at its mercy.

Action Steps for This Chapter

-Record the date on which you close each of your credit cards.

-Commit: Credit is for budgeted spends only.

-Pull your free credit report this week.

-Subscribe to mindfulness, either on or off the cusp.

-Consider a new "Fun Fund" savings account and redirect some of those BNPL purchases.

Mic-Drop Lesson

Credit is a game. Losing or winning just comes down to whether you play out of fear or you play smarter. Master it, and credit is a lever of freedom instead of a chain of debt.

Chapter 3
Stop Paying the Bank

The Real Talk

Banks are in the business of making money, and overdraft fees are one of their favorite tools. Banks in the United States collected billions of dollars in overdraft fees in 2023. Not because we're all irresponsible, but because most of us experience "money accidents." A bill passes a day sooner than expected. A deposit posts late. A small purchase sneaks through when your balance is low. Suddenly, you're hit with $35 per overdraft, sometimes more than once a day. About a year ago, I was in the midst of setting up new bank accounts, rearranging my finances, switching banks, and trying to get everything in order. Before I could finish what I'd started, life had other plans: I was unexpectedly admitted to the hospital. What happened next was, to put it mildly, a total fiasco.

The only account I'd left open at my old bank was a checking account, and I had already moved the overdraft protection and payroll deposit to the new one. As luck would have it, several payments were still presented to the old bank. To their credit, they paid every one of them, but not without handing me a very generous bill for their "kindness."

I can honestly tell you, it hurt my feelings. I had flashes of what that money could have been, at least two pairs of really good shoes sacrificed as a reward for my bank's helpfulness.

A few weeks later, I reached out to ask if they might be willing to compromise on the fees. They were polite, even a little apologetic, but in the end, it was still going to cost me the price of two pairs of heels.

Foundation Reminder:

Every overdraft fee is money you are giving away for nothing in return.

What Is an Overdraft?

Simply put, an overdraft occurs when you spend more money than is in your checking account.

Instead of declining your purchase, the bank pays for it and bills you a fat fee.

• Example: You have $50 in your checking account.

• You spend $60 on groceries.

• The bank pays it and then charges you a $35 fee.

• That grocery run did come to $95, after all. Translation: The penalty you pay for not being a robot is overdraft fees.

The Bridge Between Checking and Savings

Here's the trick few people know: You can protect yourself by associating your checking account with a savings account.

• The bank doesn't charge you $35; it takes the money from your savings instead.

• You "pay yourself back," not the bank.

• Some banks charge a small transfer fee ($5–$10), but that's still much better than $35+ per overdraft.

Foundation Tip: If your bank doesn't have overdraft protection (linking accounts), change banks.

Why Banks Love Overdrafts

• Overdraft fees are among the largest sources of profit for banks.

- They aren't concerned if it's an "accident."
- They assume customers won't realize that there's a better way.

Lesson: Don't pay for the bank's vacation. Keep your money.

What To Do Instead:

1. Establish Overdraft Protection: Connect checking → savings.
2. Create an Emergency Buffer: Leave a $100–$200 cushion in checking.
3. Use Alerts: With most banking apps, you can set balance alerts at $100, $200, or a custom number.
4. Check Posting Dates: Find Out When Bills Clear and Deposits Post.
5. Reconcile Weekly: Take 10 minutes and compare your checking activity to your budget.

The Numbers in Real Life

- One overdraft = $35. Two overdrafts/month = $70.
- Over a year = $840.

6. That's nearly $1,000 a year that could've been used to help build your emergency fund, pay off debt, or even invest.

Lesson:

Stopping your cash from slipping through accidents' fingers is just as powerful as getting more.

Faith Connection ◈ Luke 16:11 "If you are untrustworthy about worldly wealth, who will trust you with the true riches of heaven? Handling small things, such as overdraft protection, is a disciplined approach. It's a small step that could have big ripples.

Action Steps for This Chapter

Call your bank today. Ask: "Can I set up an overdraft account from another account?"

If yes → set it up. If no → think about moving banks. Set up alerts in your banking app for low balances to stay informed. Establish a $100–$200 mini buffer in your checking account. Write down how much you've paid in overdraft fees over the past year and resolve to never pay one ever again.

Mic-Drop Lesson

Overdraft fees are optional. With a phone call and some preparation, you can stop paying your bank for your money's worth and start paying yourself first.

Chapter 4
Budgeting That Works

The Real Talk

The reason most folks have anxiety toward budgeting is that it feels constraining. You create a tidy spreadsheet, plug in all the numbers, and then life comes along. It's because gas costs more this month, or you had to make an extra grocery run, or you took a road trip. Suddenly, your budget doesn't work in the real world, and you feel like a failure.

You want to know the secret no one tells you: Do NOT delete your original budget. Add an "Actual" column on your worksheet.

Why Create a Budget

Creating a budget isn't about limiting what you can have; it's about learning how to make what you have work for you.

Without a plan, money often disappears in small, unnoticed ways, what I call "financial leaks."

A budget helps you identify those leaks and redirect your resources toward things that truly matter.

Here's why a budget matters:

- It builds awareness. You can't change what you don't track.
- It creates boundaries. Boundaries protect what you value, and that includes your money.
- It builds discipline. Budgeting enhances your ability to make intentional decisions, even when emotions try to take over.
- It brings peace of mind. Knowing your bills are covered and

your goals are funded reduces financial anxiety.

Simply put, a budget turns chaos into clarity.

When to Create a Budget

The best time to create a budget is before you need one, when you're calm, focused, and ready to be proactive instead of reactive.

But if you've already hit a financial wall or are feeling stretched thin, now is the perfect time to start.

You should create or revisit your budget when:

- You experience a life change, such as a new job, marriage, relocation, or the arrival of a baby.
- You notice you're living paycheck to paycheck or frequently overdrafting.
- You're trying to pay off debt or save for a specific goal.
- You want to build wealth or invest intentionally.
- You simply want to feel more in control of your financial life.

Creating a budget isn't a one-time event; it's a living, breathing plan that evolves as your life changes.

Think of it this way: a budget isn't punishment; it's permission to tell your money how to serve your peace, your priorities, and your purpose.

Foundation Reminder:

Budgets are not about perfection. They're about awareness.

The Budgeting Lie

The myth is that budgets should always be balanced. The truth is, life doesn't balance; life is not perfect numbers. If you rig figures to close gaps, you will never see where your money really goes.

• Example: You allocate $250 for gas.

• This month, in fact, you spent $350 because of a road trip.

• Once you "rectify" your budget to $350, you have lost sight of all that extra $100.

That $100 didn't disappear. It simply remained undocumented, and undocumented money will always find a way to trickle out.

The Magic of the Actual Column Itself

There should be two numbers in your budget:

• Planned: What you expected to spend.

• Actual: What you actually spent. This does three powerful things:

1. Accountability: You know how your money was actually spent.

2. Intentionality: You discover what you really spend.

3. Clarity: This allows you to make future budgets according to true numbers.

Lesson: Truth lives in the "actual" column.

How to Build It

1. Make Categories: Housing, utilities, food, transportation, debt, savings, fun.

2. Write Planned Numbers: Best guess at the beginning of each month.

3. Monitor Real Spending: Keep track of actual spending as it occurs.

4. Compare & Reflect: Is there any area where you overspent? Where did you save? Why?

5. Modify Forward, Not Backward: Do not amend the old budget. Consider it when you plan more judiciously next time.

6. Example: The grocery overage being $100 each month isn't your fault. It's your estimate. Either increase the budget or figure out a way to reduce spending.

7. The Numbers in Real Life

• Planned: Groceries = $400.

• Actual: Groceries = $525.

• Difference: $125. Instead of guilt, you have data. Perhaps you want a meal plan, some coupons, or even fewer trips to the store. The budget isn't broken. It's showing you the truth.

Case Study: The Gas Gap. Maria would put $200 into gas each month. However, her "Actual" column read $280-$320 each month. "Instead of beating herself up, she adjusted to $300 and started carpooling and bringing her lunch," she said. In six months, she accumulated $180.

Lesson: Oh, she has the money. It revealed her real life.

Faith Connection ◈ Proverbs 27:23: "Be sure you know the condition of your flocks; pay attention to your herds." In modern parlance: know the state of your money. A budget isn't about shame. It's about stewardship.

Action Steps for This Chapter

-Establish a budget with figures for both Planned and Actual.

-Write down every expense for 30 days, no rounding up, no estimating.

-Review differences at month's end.

-Update your Planned column for Next Month based on Reality.

-Celebrate progress, not perfection.

Mic-Drop Lesson

Budgets aren't there to imprison you; they're there to liberate you. The "Actual" column is the mirror for you. It reveals the truth, and the truth will make you powerful.

Chapter 5
Checking vs. Savings

The Real Talk

"Imagine that your money is like an army. You want a base camp (that receives and dispatches resources) and a reserve unit (available when a crisis hits). For your money, that base camp is your checking account, and the reserve is your savings account.

Too many women attempt to manage everything with just one account. The result? Confusion, overdrafts, and missed opportunities. Dividing your roles between checking and savings is a source of clarity and control.

Foundation Reminder: Your checking account is for monitoring spending. Your checking account is for playing it safe.

Current Accounts

The Hub sets current accounts as the command center. A checking account is where your money resides for everyday access and transactions.

- Deposits: Your salary; transfers in; earned refunds.

- Withdrawals: Bills, debit card purchases, automated payments. It's designed for constant activity.

Types of Checking Accounts:

- Basic Checking: The generic, usually with fees.

- Free or Online Checking: Monthly fees are zero; the mobile app is key.

- Rewards Checking: Cash back, miles on airlines, or interest.

• Interest-Bearing Checking: Earns a microscopically small percentage on balances.

• Student/Teen Checking: Lower fees, basic features.

Pros of Checking Accounts (vs. Cash):

• Safety: FDIC insured up to $250,000.

• Tracking: Monthly statements help you see where your money is going.

• Tools: Direct deposit, bill pay, alerts, and budgeting features.

• Control: Serves as the central command to send money to savings, debt repayment, and investments.

Building Foundation Trick: They treat the checking account like a command station, guiding money where it needs to go rather than letting cash float around.

Savings Accounts

The Safety Net

A savings account acts as a "safety net" for your money.

A savings account is for money you do not touch very often.

• Why: Emergencies, large purchases, or a buffer for checking.

• Growth: Earns interest (usually more in online banks).

Types of Savings Accounts:

Basic Savings: Low interest, easy to open. High-Yield Savings (HYSA): Online banks that pay higher interest rates (3-5% in recent years).

Money Market Account: A Hybrid account with check writing, generally higher minimums.

Why It Matters:

• Protects and divides your money.

• Stop dipping into your emergency fund.

• May be connected to a checking account to prevent overdraft fees.

Smart Move: Use your savings account as a backup for overdraft protection. Pay yourself, not the bank.

The Checking + Savings Partnership

Think of these accounts as partners, not competitors.

• Reconciling = Command: Pay bills, monitor inflows/outflows.

• Savings = Shield: Guard against the unexpected and work toward what you want. Example:

• $1,200 rent → Checking. • $400 groceries → Checking.

• Automatic $50 a month transfer → Savings.

• Checking takes care of the hustle, and savings quietly add up in the background.

The Numbers in Real Life

• Checking balance = $2,000.

• $500 → Savings for unexpected expenses.

• Bills knocked off = $1,200 rent, $400 for groceries, and $200 in utilities.

- End of month: Checking = $200 cushion, Savings = $500 shield.

Translation: You lived, you paid bills, and yet your wealth continued to grow.

Reconciling Your Bank Account

We were having a family discussion the other day, and I asked my nephew if he knew what a check was. He laughed and said, "Yeah, but I use my card for everything." So I asked him another question: "Do you reconcile your checking account or even your savings account, for that matter?" He looked away and said, "No one ever told me to." So I followed up: "Then how do you know if transactions you didn't authorize were paid? Have you ever had a returned transaction? Do you know if your bank is charging you a fee?" He shrugged. "I have no idea, nothing's been declined yet." And that's when it hit me: so many people were never taught how to reconcile an account.

◈ Let's Talk About How to Reconcile Your Bank Account

Whether it's checking or savings, reconciling simply means making sure your records match the bank's records. It's financial hygiene like brushing your teeth, but for your money.

Here's how you do it step by step:

Step 1: Gather Your Records

- Your bank statement (monthly or digital).

- Your own list of transaction receipts, app logs, or your notes.

Step 2: Match Every Transaction

Go line by line through your statement:

- Check that every deposit you made shows up.

• Confirm that every purchase or payment listed is one you actually made.

• Circle or flag any that you don't recognize that could be fraud or an error.

Step 3: Watch for Bank Fees Banks often charge for overdrafts, maintenance, or transfers, and these fees can quietly eat into your money.

� Make note of any fees.

� If they don't make sense, call your bank.

Step 4: Record Missing Transactions. If you have written a check or made a payment that hasn't cleared yet, please note it. That money is still technically gone from your account, even if it hasn't shown up yet.

Step 5: Adjust Your Balance. Take your ending balance on the statement. Then add or subtract anything that hasn't cleared. This gives you your true balance, not just what the app says.

Why It Matters

• You catch fraud early.

• You stay aware of your real balance (not what's left after pending payments).

• You avoid surprise overdrafts or fees.

• And most importantly, you build the habit of owning your money.

If no one ever told you to reconcile your account, consider this your sign. Financial freedom doesn't start with how much you make; it starts with knowing where your money goes.

Case Study: One small adjustment,

The Emergency Backup

Diane used to cover $300-$400/year in overdraft fees. After losing the needle in the haystack, she connected her checking to her savings, the equivalent of a slap across the face. After one "oops" purchase, the bank routed $25 from her savings account to her checking account to cover the "oops" purchase instead of eating $35 in overdraft fees. In a year, that small change saved her hundreds of dollars.

Lesson: Savings is not just for long-term goals. It's also about preserving your today.

Faith Connection ⟐ Proverbs 21:5: "The plans of the diligent lead to profit as surely as haste leads to poverty." It is fidelity to divide your money into roles. It's the plan that keeps chaos at bay.

Action Steps for This Chapter

-If your bank charges a monthly fee, open a free checking account.

-Open (or transfer into) a high-yield savings account for more robust growth.

-Connect savings to checking for overdraft protection.

-Automate a transfer ($25–$100/month) to savings.

-Checking for spending, savings for safety, and no crossovers.

Chapter 5A.
Making Your Money Work for You

The Real Talk

"As a single parent with young children, having extra money in a checking account, you know, "just in case," seems like a foreign concept for many women. It feels safe, but here's the issue: checking accounts don't make your money grow; they hold it. More often than not, it comes with no interest, no rewards, and lots of fees if you're not careful. This is where a zero-balance checking account (ZBCA) comes into play. Rather than leaving your money dormant in a checking account, a zero balance account lets you put every dollar to work.

Reminder: money is a job. If it stays in one place, it's unemployed.

What Is a Zero Balance Account? A zero balance checking account (ZBCA) is a checking or money market account with a maintained balance of $0.

Here's how it works:

• Your checking account is tied to a funding account (typically savings or your main operating account).

• When you write a check, swipe your debit card, or pay a bill, just the right amount of money automatically moves between your funding account and a checking account in order to cover the transaction.

• The bottom line is, any excess cash sweeps back into your funding account at the end of the day.

Translation: You only store money where it earns, not where it idles.

How to Set One Up

1. Ask Your Bank or Credit Union. Not all institutions offer true zero-balance checking, but many larger, business-friendly banks do. Some will help you set up a sweep arrangement between accounts.

2. Link to a Funding Account

◦ Main option: A savings account (preferably high yield).

◦ Alternative: A money market account, or even an investment sweep.

3. Set Transaction Rules

◦ Define how many moves per transaction (exact or rounded).

◦ Decide if funds sweep back daily, weekly, or monthly.

4. Automate It Once set, you don't have to touch it. Your checking works like a pass-through tool, not a storage container.

Pros of a Zero Balance Checking Account

Maximizes Growth: Keeps your money in savings or investments where it can earn interest.

Prevents Idle Cash: No extra $500 "just sitting" in checking, doing nothing.

Simplifies Cash Flow: Transactions are clean, with all surplus swept back.

Reduces Temptation: Less "easy access" money means you're less likely to overspend.

Cons of a Zero-Balance Checking Account

Bank Fees: Some banks charge for ZBCA (Zero Balance Checking Account) services.

Always ask. Overdraft Risks:

If the sweep doesn't happen fast enough or your funding account is low, you could overdraft. Set up Limits: Smaller banks or online-only banks may not offer them.

Learning Curve: Takes discipline and tracking to get used to seeing "$0" every day without panicking.

Why Use One?

Because a checking account is not an investment tool. It's a highway; money should pass through, not park there.

With a zero balance system:

• Your savings grow faster because money stays there until needed.

• Your budget becomes clearer; you only see what you spend.

• Your financial control sharpens; no more foggy "where did that extra cash go?"

Example: If you normally keep $2,000 in checking "just in case," moving that to a high-yield savings account at 4.5% interest = an extra $90/year for doing nothing. Multiply that over the years, and it adds up.

Faith Connection ◈ Matthew 25:27: "You should have put my money on deposit with the bankers, so that when I returned, I would have received it back with interest." Even in scripture, idle money wasn't praised. The goal is stewardship, putting money where it multiplies, not where it stagnates.

Action Steps for This Chapter

1. Call your bank and ask: "Do you offer zero balance checking or sweep accounts?"

2. Open a high-yield savings account if you don't already have one.

3. Start small: Keep $100 in checking, sweep everything else into savings weekly.

4. Track results after 3 months; notice how much more you've saved.

5. Re-frame your mindset: Checking is a pass-through; savings is the builder.

Mic-Drop Lesson

A zero balance checking account isn't about having "nothing." It's about putting every dollar to work. Stop letting money nap in checking; make it work for you."

Chapter 5B.

Zero Balance Checking + Overdraft Protection

Make Your Money Work For You Trick: Zero Balance Checking + Overdraft Protection.

The Problem Without It

• Zero balance checking works by sweeping money in/out.

• But if your sweep doesn't trigger in time or your funding account is low, your checking account could show "$0" when a bill hits.

• Without protection, that means NSF (non-sufficient funds) fees, which are often $25–$40 per transaction.

Translation: A tool meant to save you money could end up costing you.

The Solution:

Link the Zero Balance account to an Overdraft Account. Many banks allow you to link your checking account, providing a backup account.

Here's how to match it up: Zero balance checking:

1. Link Funding Account (Primary)

◦ Your checking is already connected to a savings or money market that does the daily sweep.

2. Add a Backup Overdraft Account (Second Line of Defense)

◦ Could be another savings account, small line of credit, or linked credit card.

◦ If the zero balance sweep fails or falls short, and you have written something above zero on the account, then overdraft coverage comes in as automatic again.

3. Set Priorities

◦ There is daily funding on the primary sweep.

◦ 2nd overdraft = for emergencies only.

◦ This saves NSF fees while your money can keep working.

Pros of Adding Overdraft Protection

No NSF Fees:

No longer rely on a traditional account to protect you from fees and mistakes.

Extra Safety: You're still protected if your funding account runs out.

Peace of Mind-Zero balance is for everyone, carefree service.

Cons to Watch Out For

Transfer Fees: Some banks charge transfer fees of up to $10–$12 per overdraft transfer, even with protection.

Interest Risk: If your overdraft is part of a credit card or line of credit, interest charges apply.

The Perils of False Security: Reliance on overdraft increasingly leaves you papering over the cash flow cracks.

Best Practice Setup

• Starting point (i.e., primary sweep account): High-yield savings.

• Back-up overdraft account: Tiny savings cushion OR line of credit (with little or no fees).

Tip: Request that your bank waive overdraft transfer fees; many will if you hold other accounts with them.

Example:

• Bill hits: $200.

• ZBCA sweep: $180 (oops, we fell a little short on that saving).

• Overdraft protection: covers the $20 shortage.

• You pay yourself back for your overdraft rather than the bank's standard $35 NSF fee.

Why It's Smart

Checking balance of zero keeps your $$ working harder. Overdraft protection is a way of guarding against errors that don't come cheaply. Together, they've developed a system that is efficient and safe.

Mic-Drop Lesson:

Overdraft protection can also be linked to a zero-balance checking account. Think of them as the airbags in your car; you don't ever want to use them, but when something happens in a crash, they will save you.

Chapter 5C.

How to Create a Savings Account for Overdraft Protection

The First Question: "How can I have a savings account to use for overdraft protection at all?" It's a fair question. If things are tight, socking away more never seems realistic. But here's the kicker: you don't need a large change; you need a small but consistent one.

The Coffee Example

- $6 coffee per day × 5 days = $30 a week.
- $30 per week × 4 weeks = $120 per month.
- $120 a month × 1 year = $1,440 saved.

Translation: One little compromise fuels your overdraft account (and then some).

Simple Way to Execute

-Open a Separate Savings Account

◦ And label it "Overdraft Protection Fund."

◦ Attach it to your checking account.

-Redirect Coffee Money

◦ Instead of going out for coffee every day, make it at home 3x/week.

◦ Immediately transfer the $18 you would have spent into your savings account.

-Automate the Transfer

◦ Schedule a $20 weekly automatic transfer from checking to savings.

◦ This makes the habit stick.

-Watch It Grow

◦ In 3 months, you will have ~$240.

◦ You'll have ~$480 in 6 months.

◦ In one year, you will have ~$960.

That's sufficient for an overdraft cushion and a good start to saving.

Why This Works

- This isn't about extracting joy from your life; it's about balance.
- You enjoy coffee, but not every day.
- You've taken a daily habit and turned it into your safety net.

Mic-Drop Lesson:

Your overdraft protection account isn't from "leftover money." It's spawned from little compromises that move cash into savings. One cup of coffee at a time.

Chapter 6
Simple vs. Compound Interest

The Real Talk

If you've ever wondered why some people can steadily grow their wealth while others feel trapped, the answer often comes down to one thing: compound interest. None of us was ever taught the difference between simple and compound interest. The banks, the credit card companies, and the lenders know it, and they make billions on our ignorance. But once you run the numbers, you'll never look at your money quite the same way again.

Foundation Reminder:

You do not work only to earn money, but more importantly, your money can also work for you.

What Is Simple Interest?

Simple interest is when you earn (or owe) interest on the amount of your principal.

- Formula: Principal × Rate × Time.

- Example: You deposit $1,000 at 5% interest for three years by simple interest.

  - $50/year x 3 years = $150 received.

  - Total = $1,150.

Easy math, predictable outcome.

What Is Compound Interest?

Compound interest is what happens when you earn (or owe) interest on the principal amount and also on any interest you've already earned.

- Formula: Principal × (1 + Rate) ^ Time.

- Illustration: You deposit $1,000 at 5% compounded annually for 3 years.

◦ Year 1: $1,000 → $1,050.

◦ Year 2: $1,050 → $1,102.50.

◦ Year 3: $1,102.50 → $1,157.63.

◦ Total = $1,157.63.

Translation: Your money earns money, and then your earnings earn even more.

The Numbers in Real Life

- Simple interest (3 years, 5 percent): $1,150.

- Compound interest (3 years, 5 percent): $1,157.63. The difference may seem minor at first: just $7.63 more. But spread it across decades and bigger sums, and the disparity mushrooms.

For example, if you have $200/month to invest at 7% compound interest over the course of 30 years, the result is $244,000+.

The Way Debt Uses Compound Interest Against You.

Compound interest isn't reserved for savings and investment vehicles; it works against you with credit cards, too.

- Example: $1,000 balance on a 20% interest rate.

- Pay the minimum → it could take 5+ years to pay off.

• Interest paid = $500+ of the interest.

Lesson: The math that grows your savings can also grow your debt. The distinction is whether you're a borrower or a lender. Many men are taught to start investing even $25 a month as early as their 20s. Women frequently are forced to wait until they have the luxury of "things settling down." The reality is that time, not sum, matters more.

• Example: Begin investing $100/month at 25 → $228,000 by 65.

• Do the same at 35 → $113,000 by 65.

The change is a matter of time, not money.

Faith Connection: ⍰ Matthew 25:21: "Thou hast been faithful with a few things, I will make thee ruler over many things." Compound interest is just one modern expression of this fact: being faithful with little has a way over time of becoming huge.

Action Steps for This Chapter

-Get a savings or investment account that generates compound interest.

-Begin where you're at, even if it's just $25/month.

-List one debt of yours that is compounding with interest. Create a strategy to pay it down as quickly as you can.

-Tell a young one about the principle of compound interest; start early.

-Resolve: I will make compound interest my leverage, not the other way around.

Chapter 7
The Real Cost of Lifestyle Choices

The Real Talk

Big purchases such as cars, houses, and vacations are what we assume break our budgets. However, the truth is that all too often, it's the little decisions we make every day that quietly siphon off our funds. A $6 coffee. A $12 lunch. An impromptu takeout night when you're too exhausted to cook. None of them feels huge in the moment, but if you stack them up over weeks and months, they add up to thousands.

Foundation Reminder: Little leaks sink big ships.

The Coffee Example

• Daily coffee shop habit = $6 x 5 days/week = $30/week.

• Over a month = ~$120.

• Over a year = $1,440. Translation: That "small treat" is a plane ticket, payment on your credit card or hotel bill, or a chunk of your emergency fund.

The Eating Out Example

• Dinner out = $40 per person, $100+ for family.

• Two days a week = $400 to $500 per month.

• One year = $5,000–$6,000.

Lesson: You could actually be eating up your nest egg.

The Meal Plan Shift: Don't deprive yourself altogether, but instead make thoughtful choices.

-Plan a Weekly Menu: Choose 4–5 potential meals that you are sure you will actually cook.

- Shop by List: Avoid impulse purchases.
- Batch Cook or Prep Ahead: Makes those "too tired to cook" nights easier!
- Use Coupons & Apps: Several grocery stores and apps (Ibotta, Rakuten) reward you with cash. Example: $100 a month in savings on groceries = $1,200/year → invested for 10 years at 7% growth = over $16,000.
- The Numbers in Real Life

• Coffee + dining out regularly = $500 a month = $6,000 a year.

• If it's invested at 7% for 20 years = $246,000. What the actual cost is not just money today but wealth tomorrow.

Case Study: The Grocery Swap Tina and her children used to dine out 3–4 nights weekly, at a total of ~$600/month. She began meal planning and restricted dining out to once a week. Savings: $400/month. She paid off a $4,800 credit card balance in one year.

Lesson: Pulling back wasn't deprivation; it was freedom from debt.

Freedom Tip

This is not about trimming every joy. It's about the question: "Does this purchase allow me to live according to my wealth story?" If it does, keep it. If it doesn't, redirect it.

Faith Connection ⟐ Proverbs 21:17 (NIV) "Whoever loves pleasure will become poor; whoever loves wine and olive oil will never be rich."

The Bible is not saying 'don't enjoy life'; it's saying 'don't eat so much that you deprive yourself in the future.'

Action Steps for This Chapter

-Monitor one week of "small" spending (coffee, lunches, takeout).

-Multiply that number by 12 to get the yearly cost.

-Make one plan this week and stick to it.

-Choose one expense (coffee, lunch, eating out for dinner) to halve this month.

-Re-allocate savings to go toward your emergency fund or debt repayment.

Mic-Drop Lesson

Rich isn't always just about what you make. It can be as much about what you retain. A coffee here and a takeout night there may not seem like big deals, but eventually, together they could end up costing you six figures in lost wealth.

Chapter 8
Saving for Major Purchases

The Real Talk

Few of us ever learned how to save up for big purchases. What we were not educated about was how to pay for them. New car? Take out a loan. Dream home? Stretch for the highest mortgage you can "afford." Furniture, appliances, vacations swipe the card, sign the papers, and worry later about how you're going to pay the bill. Here's the reality: All loans have a hidden cost in the form of interest. And each time you forego saving in order to borrow, you are making someone else wealthy instead of yourself.

Foundation Reminder: Deciding if you can afford the payment is not the question. The question is: "Can I afford to buy it?"

Why Saving Beats Borrowing

• No Interest: Cash buyers don't owe lenders any added interest.

• More Negotiating Power: When you come to the table, sellers will take you seriously.

• Financial Freedom: You own the asset, not the liability. Example: Purchase a $20,000 car with a 6% loan for 60 months —> pay $3,200+ in interest. (And you can buy the credit equivalent of that same car directly with the savings → $3,200 in your pocket.)

How to Build a Purchase Fund

-Define the Goal

◦ Car? Home? Vacation? Wedding?

◦ Write down the target cost.

-Set a Timeline

◦ Car in 3 years? Home in 5? Vacation in 12 months?

◦ Cost divided by Months = Monthly Savings specific. For example: $15,000 car in 3 years → $417/mo.

-Create a Separate Account

◦ Open a HYSA specifically for this goal.

◦ Call it "Car Fund" or "Home Fund."

-Automate Contributions

◦ Treat savings like a bill. Set up automatic transfers.

-Add Windfalls

◦ Tax refunds, bonuses, side hustle income → dump it directly into the fund.

Cars: The Depreciating Asset

The second you drive off the lot, cars lose value.

- New car: 20–30% in the first year.
- Better choice: Purchase used, well-maintained cars.
- Savings strategy: Start a car fund to avoid going into high-interest debt for an auto loan.

Lesson: Cars are not investments but liabilities. Don't overpay for status. Homes: The Equity Builder Homes are different. Cars depreciate; homes tend to appreciate over time.

But here's the key:

• The more money you are able to put down, the less of a loan you will need.

• Additional payments to principal create equity more quickly.

• Positive housing equity is another potential source of emergency cash (HELOC, refinance).

Smart move: Shoot for 20% down to avoid PMI (private mortgage insurance).

Other Major Purchases

• Furniture & Appliances: Your first or second choice. BNPL (Buy Now, Pay Later) = DEBT.

• Vacations: Make a "travel sinking fund." Good times shouldn't leave you with debt.

• Weddings: Budget early. A wedding without debt is a more solid beginning for marriage.

The Numbers in Real Life

• Borrow $10,000 for furniture at 10% = $2,700 in interest over 5 years.

• Save $200 a month for 4 years = $9,600 in cash. Buy what you want, interest-free. Translation: Saving is delayed happiness.

Borrowing is delayed regret.

Case Study: The Shift in Buying Cars Alex had always rolled negative equity into her new car loans. At 35, she decided to take a different approach: she opened a Car Fund and paid for her next car with cash.

She avoided $6,000 in interest on the debt and began channeling that money into an investment account.

Lesson: One mindset shift can change your whole money story.

Faith Connection ◈ Romans 13:8: "Let no debt remain outstanding, except the continuing debt to love one another." Big buys don't have to equal major debt. When you save first, you honor your future self.

Action Steps for This Chapter

-Make a note of your next big purchase target.

-Divide the total cost by how many months are left until your designated date.

-Open up a dedicated high-yield savings account.

-Automate contributions like a bill.

-Direct all windfalls to this account.

Mic-Drop Lesson

Big-ticket purchases don't necessarily need to keep you chained to debt. With a plan, you can buy big while holding on to your freedom.

Chapter 9
Credit Reports & Monitoring

The Real Talk

Your credit report is more than a score; it's your financial reputation. It's a way of telling lenders, landlords, and sometimes even employers how you'll handle money. But there's the rub: too many people never see it. They figure it's "fine" until they're rejected for a loan or high interest rate, or when they learn that someone has been using their identity.

Foundation Reminder: If you don't watch your credit, someone else will and not always for the good. What Is a Credit Report? A credit report is a record of your history of borrowing and repaying.

It includes:

• Personal info: Name, address, Social Security number.

• Credit accounts: Cards, loans, mortgages.

• History of payments: On time versus late.

• Balances & limits: The amount you owe compared with your credit limit.

• Questions: Who's pulled your credit?

• Public records: Bankruptcies, collections, judgments.

Key Point: Your credit score is built based on your credit report. Clean report = stronger score.

How to Obtain Your Free Credit Report

You are entitled by law to one free report per year from each of the three major bureaus:

- Equifax
- Experian
- TransUnion

Go to AnnualCreditReport.com, the only government-approved site.

Smart Strategy: Space requests (one bureau every 4 months) to monitor year-round.

Credit Monitoring: What You Need to Know

Credit monitoring services continually monitor your credit for changes and alert you.

Free Options:

- Credit Karma
- Experian app
- Some banks and credit cards

Paid Options (more features):

- Identity theft protection
- Insurance to cover losses from fraud

Foundation Tip: Employ at least one free monitoring service.

The Numbers in Real Life

- It takes an average of 33 hours to resolve identity theft, and victims say they spend an average of $1,300 out of pocket.

• Scam accounts can destroy your credit rating and cost thousands more in higher loan rates.

• The difference between a quick fix and years of remediation usually comes down to catching the fraud early.

How to Shield Your Credit Identity

1. Monitor Reports On a Regular Basis: Watch for mistakes or early signs of fraud.

2. Dispute Errors: You are entitled to contest inaccurate data.

3. Freeze Your Credit (Optional): Stops new accounts from being opened in your name.

4. Alerts: Receive alerts for new inquiries or changes to balances.

5. Protect Personal Info: Shred documents, have robust passwords, look out for phishing.

Reminder: You're the first line of defense for your financial reputation.

Case Study: The Stolen Identity Jasmine applied for a car loan and was horrified to discover that several cards had been opened in her name, accounts she had never utilized. It took months to dispute her credit and make the necessary repairs. If she had been watching, she would have learned of the fraud in a matter of days, not months.

Lesson: Keeping an eye on your credit is not paranoia. It's protection.

Faith Connection ◈ Proverbs 4:23: "Above all else, guard your heart, for everything you do flows from it. Your heart directs your life. Your credit determines your financial possibilities. Both need guarding.

Action Steps for This Chapter

Visit AnnualCreditReport.com and draw one bureau's report today. Put a special emphasis on errors or accounts that you don't recall. If you feel vulnerable, consider opting for a free credit freeze.

Mic-Drop Lesson

Your credit report is your financial good name. Protect it as you would your name, because once broken, it is almost impossible to mend. Subscribe to at least one free monitoring service.

Mark a calendar to check another bureau in 4 months.

Chapter 10

Debt, What It Is, How It Works, and How to Break Free

The Real Talk

Debt is one of the most significant barriers to achieving financial security. Earnings mean nothing if your credit card companies, car loans, and personal loans are siphoning off too much of them; I can assure you that you will forever feel like everything is consistently three steps behind.

Here's the fact: debt is more than numbers on a page. It's a weight. It's stress. It's lost opportunities. But the good news? Debt is also solvable. Once you figure out how it operates, there's no effort to escape.

Foundation Reminder: As costs increase, debt becomes expensive, not only in terms of money, but also in other ways. It costs peace of mind.

What Debt Really Is: Debt = the money you borrow today for the promise of repayment tomorrow plus interest.

Types of debt:

- Credit Cards: High-interest, revolving balances.
- Auto Loans: Secured by your car, typically 3 to 7 years.
- Mortgages: These are secured by your home and generally last 15 to 30 years.
- Student Loans: Education-related, payments often postponed.
- Personal Loans: Unsecured and on the basis of credit score.

Key Point: Not all debt is "bad." But there is always an expense.

How Interest Works Against You

- Example: $5,000 credit card balance with a 20% interest rate.

- Minimum payment: $100/month.

- Time to pay off: 7 years.

- Total paid: $8,400. ◈ Translation: You borrowed $5,000 and returned an additional $3,400, but left with nothing. The Debt Trap: Easy to get in (credit offers, loans, BNPL apps). Difficult to get out (interest + fees compound). Induces dependency (you spend your income before it arrives). Debt takes away tomorrow's income to pay for yesterday's choices.

How To Free Yourself: Two Strategies That Work

- Debt Snowball

◦ Pay off bite-sized balance early for the easy win.

◦ Rollover that payment into the next debt.

◦ Builds momentum and confidence.

- Debt Avalanche

◦ Pay the highest-interest debt first.

◦ Saves more money long-term.

◦ It will require some discipline to stay with it. Whether one works better than the other just depends.

Practical Steps to Escape Debt

These debts will include your balance, the interest rate, and a minimum payment amount. Choose Snowball or Avalanche. Do not take on new debt (cut cards if necessary). Create a mini emergency fund ($500–$1,000) so that the unexpected doesn't bite you back. Automate payments where possible. Rejoice in Milestones: Each paid-off debt is a raise.

The Numbers in Real Life

• Paying $300 a month on a $10,000 credit card balance at 20% → ~4 years to pay off, and you'd pay about $6,000 in interest.

• Raise to $500/month → paid off in about two years, $2,000 interest.

Lesson: The sooner you tackle debt, the more freedom you purchase.

Case Study: From Trapped to Free

For years, Angela carried credit card debt of $15,000 and paid the minimums. In the end, she said she followed Dave Ramsey's Snowball method and paid off that $800 card first, then simply rolled it from one creditor to the next. She was debt-free in 3 years and funneling $600/ month into savings. Lesson: Progress, not perfection, is how you win the debt war.

Faith Connection ◈ Proverbs 22:7: "The borrower is servant to the lender." Debt is bondage. To break free is to be unshackled not only financially, but spiritually and emotionally.

Action Steps for This Chapter

-List every debt you have.

-Don't hide from the numbers.

-Select Snowball or Avalanche and orbit your initial target.

-Establish a $500–$1,000 emergency fund to avoid backsliding.

-Trim spending to find more money for extra payments.

-Put it on a calendar when you will be debt-free and look at that date daily.

Mic-Drop Lesson

Debt handcuffs your future to your past. Breaking free gets you back control of your money and your life.

Chapter 11
Emergency Funds

The Real Talk

Life can be full of surprises. The car breaks down. A child gets sick. Hours are cut at work. All too often, such surprises end up as debt because there's no cushion in reserve. That's where the emergency fund fits in. It's not glamorous, and it won't make you rich. But it's the shield that prevents a surprise from turning into a financial catastrophe.

Foundation Reminder: Not if, but when.

What Is an Emergency Fund?

An emergency fund is a designated amount of money set aside for unexpected expenses. It's not for vacations, holiday shopping, or "treat yourself" splurges. It's for life's unplanned hits.

Examples of True Emergencies:

- Medical bills.
- Car repairs.
- Job loss or reduced hours.
- Home fixes (leaky roof, broken furnace).

Test: If it's urgent, important, and unexpected, it counts.

How Much Do You Need?

- Starter Fund: $500 to $1,000 to break the debt cycle.

• Next Step: 3–6 months of living expenses once you're out from under debt.

• Long-Term Goal: 9 to 12 months if you are self-employed or have a single income.

Example: If your monthly expenses are $3,000, then shoot for $9,000–$18,000.

Where to Keep It

• High-Yield Savings Account (HYSA): Safe, liquid, and it earns interest.

• Work Account: Do not mix with spending money.

• Available, but Not Too Well Done: You want to get there quickly, but not by swiping it with your debit card on a whim.

Avoid: Speaking of which, don't invest it in stocks or tie it up in CDs unless emergencies require swift cash.

Why It Matters

Without an emergency fund:

• A $600 car repair = one credit card swipe = months of debt.

• With an emergency fund: You pay cash and walk away.

Translation: Your safety cushion buys peace.

The Numbers in Real Life

• 57 percent of Americans would be unable to pay a $1,000 emergency expense.

• Average credit card interest = 20 percent.

• One emergency can set off a debt spiral for years to come.

Your emergency fund is a firewall between you and financial hell.

Case Study: How The Shield Works

Monica lost her job unexpectedly. Because she had $9,000 in her emergency fund, enough to cover three months of expenses, she could afford to keep a roof over her head, pay bills, and look for another job without stress. By month 4, she had a new job and was still debt-free.

Lesson: Her emergency fund transformed a disaster into an inconvenience.

Faith Connection ◈ Proverbs 6:6–8: "Go to the ant, you sluggard; consider its ways and be wise! It prepares its sustenance in summer, seasoning and storing it in the harvest. Storing up beforehand is not fear; it's wisdom.

Action Steps for This Chapter

-Open up a separate savings account specifically for emergencies.

-Your top priority should be to save your first $500-$1,000 as fast as you can.

-Create an automatic transfer ($25–$100/month) until you reach 3–6 months' expenses.

-You should replenish your emergency fund as soon as you draw it down.

-Write your "why": what are the elements of security this fund will bring to your life?

Mic-Drop Lesson

An emergency fund isn't going to make you rich, but it will prevent you from becoming broke. It is more than money; it is peace and stability and confidence to handle the curve balls that life inevitably throws you.

How to Save Your First $500 (Faster Than You Think)

How to Save Your First $500 (Quicker Than You Think) When cash is tight or nonexistent, saving $500 may seem entirely out of reach. But here's the reality: $500 is not strictly about making more; it's just redirecting and creating opportunities. Here are some simple, achievable steps to help you reach your goal:

Sell Stuff You Don't Need (Garage sale, Online, etc.)

• Take a tour through closets, your garage, and your kitchen cabinets.

• Sell clothes, furniture, tools, or electronics you no longer use.

• Consider apps such as Facebook Marketplace, Poshmark, OfferUp, and eBay.

Potential: $100 to $300 over a weekend.

Start a Side Gig

• Walk dogs, babysit, or run errands: Sign up with TaskRabbit, Rover, or Care.com.

• Teach or freelance your skills online (Upwork, Fiverr, LinkedIn).

• Become a delivery driver for DoorDash, Uber Eats, or Instacart.

Possibility: A few hundred dollars for a few evenings.

Cut a Regular Expense for One Month

• Cancel or pause a subscription (streaming, gym, apps).

• Eat at home rather than dining out.

• Make coffee at home instead of buying one each day. Possible: $50–$150 in savings over 30 days.

De-clutter for Cash

• Bring old phones, tablets, or computers to an ecoATM or trade-in service.

• Trade in unused gift cards (sites like Card Cash). Best gift price point: $50–$100, you forgot you had.

Use "Unexpected Money"

• Tax refund? Save $100 immediately.

• Work bonus? Reallocate a slice before spending it.

• Loose change? Leverage apps like Acorns to round up your purchases and save.

Potential: $100+ without even touching your paycheck.

The Fast-Track Plan

Combine 2–3 of these tactics, and it won't take you long to reach $500:

• Sell unused items: $200

• Side gig for 2 weeks: $200

• Eliminate one cost for a month: $100 = $500 total

Mic-Drop Lesson:

Finding $500 doesn't require a raise. You have to be creative, disciplined, and carry it through. Once you build it one time, you know how to build it next time.

Chapter 12
Creating Positive Equity

The Real Talk

Equity is what you really "own" of an asset. The greater your positive equity, the more options you have.

Foundation Reminder

Debt is bleeding you, everyone. Equity empowers you.

What Is Equity? Equity = Value of Assets – Total Debt.

• If you're sitting in your house, which is worth $250,000, and have a mortgage of $180,000 →, you have $70,000 of equity.

• If your car is worth $20,000 and you owe $15,000 →, you own $5,000. Equity = ownership. Debt = obligation. Positive vs. Negative Equity

• Positive Equity: Asset is worth more than what you owe.

• Negative Equity: You owe more than the asset is worth.

Example (Car Loan):

• Car value: $18,000.

• Loan balance: $22,000.

• Equity: – $4,000 → negative equity (known colloquially as "underwater"). Negative equity traps you.

Positive equity frees you.

Why Positive Equity Matters

• Emergency Cash: Back-up options provided by home equity (HELOC, refinance).

• Money to Spend: You can sell without getting trapped.

• Wealth Builder: Homes with increasing equity tend to be stepping stones for bigger things as time passes. Whenever an asset is funded with positive equity, your money is working inside the asset (and not against it).

How to Build Positive Equity

Make a Larger Down Payment

◦ Home: Try to put 20% down to reduce debt and stay away from PMI(private mortgage insurance).

◦ Car: Most car buyers hesitate to throw money down because, let's be real, the car is a deteriorating asset, a thing that loses value the second you leave the lot.

And it's true: on average, a new car drops 10–15% of its market value instantaneously and up to 20–30% in the first year. But here's the kicker: a down payment doesn't combat depreciation; it guards you from it. When you put cash down, you'll take out fewer out-of-pocket amounts. This reduces your installment and interest on the loan. You tilt the equity in the asset. This is the difference between the car's market value and the loan amount. Without a down payment, you end up upside down, owing more than the property's market value. You face a negative selling outlook.

Example:

• $30,000 car with $0 down → you owe $30,000 + interest, but it's worth $26,000 after a week. You're instantly $4,000 upside down.

• $30,000 car with $3,000 down → you owe $27,000 on a $26,000 car. You're nearly at break-even from day one, and your payments are lower.

Pay Extra Toward Principal

◦ Making just one extra mortgage payment a year could cut years off that loan.

◦ Small extra car payments allow you to reach ownership sooner.

Choose Assets Wisely

◦ Purchase cars for reliability, not status.

◦ Purchase homes in markets that are not stagnant or declining.

Maintain the Asset

◦ Save on Maintenance = Increased Resale Value.

◦ Neglect = faster depreciation.

The Numbers in Real Life

• Home: $200,000 mortgage at 30 years and a 6% interest rate.

◦ An additional $100/month → 5 years less on loan, nearly $40,000 interest saved.

• Car: $20,000 loan at 7%.

◦ Pay $50/month more → reduce the loan by 1 year and save ~$800 in interest.

Translation: By making extra payments, you create (or build) equity, which will save you money in the long run.

Case Study: The Car Flip

Marcus purchased a secondhand car for $15,000 and put $5,000 as a down payment. And two years later, he owed just $7,000, but the car was still valued at $12,000. That $5,000 slice of positive equity let him sell and trade up without rolling debt forward.

Lesson: Cars depreciate, but you can own them intelligently.

Faith Connection ◈ Deuteronomy 28:12: "The Lord will open the heavens, the storehouse of his bounty. Thou shalt lend unto many nations, and thou shalt not borrow." Positive equity is a 21st-century expression of living into that promise, owning more than you owe.

Action Steps for This Chapter

-Record the value and loan balance of your home or car.

-Determine your equity (Value – Debt).

-If it is negative, establish a structured payoff schedule of beliefs.

-If it is positive, preserve it by holding the asset.

-Make one extra payment toward the principal this year.

Mic-Drop Lesson

Having an asset with debt isn't the same as having wealth. It's positive equity that transforms houses and cars from financial sponges into financial soldiers.

Chapter 13
Tithing Time, Talent, and Treasure

The Real Talk

What I hear from most people, when they talk about tithing, is that they only think of money. And yes, that does include financial giving. But real wealth and true generosity aren't about writing a check. It's a way of living with an open hand, giving of your time, your talents, and your treasure. Tithing is not just about money but about how our generosity points beyond itself. It's about constructing it in others.

Foundation Reminder:

Tithing is about giving, not just money.

Time: The Currency Everyone

You may not always think you have extra cash to spare, but odds are good that you can find time.

- Volunteering at a hospital or community shelter.
- Babysitting for a non-coupled parent.
- Sharing a budgeting or cooking lesson with kids in your neighborhood.

Lesson: Your time is valuable. Spend it where it leverages impact.

Talent: What You Already Have

There is something we all know or do well. It might be budgeting, car repair, cooking, organizing, or teaching. To share that skill is a way for others to build wealth.

- Guide a free workshop if you can budget.

- If you're car-smart, volunteer to help friends and neighbors choose better when they buy or service.

- If you like to cook, teach someone how to plan meals on a budget.

Sample: One hour of teaching will prevent another person from hundreds if not thousands.

Treasure: The Money You Steward

Yes, money matters. Fellowship money supports your church, nonprofits, and life-changing causes. But giving is not merely about generosity; it's also about point of view.

- It's a sign that money is a tool, not your master.

- It's a lesson in discipline and intentionality.

- It gets your wealth story in sync with your values.

Freedom Tip: Even if you do it little by little, more frequent giving trains your heart to be completely free of fear and lack.

The Numbers in Real Life

- 1 hour a week of tutoring → helps a child pass classes and dream bigger.

- Teach 5 women how to budget → They save each $1,000/year = a total of $5,000 impact.

- Invest 10% of income → provides for missions, communities, and future generations.

Translation: Generosity begets more than meets the eye.

Case Study: The Gift of the Car Strategist gets texts and calls when someone is buying or servicing a car. Why? Because I know the industry. That, for me, is a way of tithing my talent, helping others to avoid traps and to save money. That's as valuable as writing a check for me.

Lesson: The best gift isn't always money; sometimes, it's knowledge.

Faith Connection ◈ Malachi 3:10:"Bring ye all the tithes into the storehouse, that there may be meat in mine house. Try me now in this, says the Lord Almighty, and see if I will not open for you the windows of heaven. God's economy works differently. When you do give up, you don't lose; you make room for overflow.

Action Steps for This Chapter

-Spot one slice of time you can donate this month.

-Journal a talent that you possess, which you can share to help others create wealth or stability.

-Choose a regular percentage cut of treasure (money) that you will offer, even if it's tiny.

-Teach someone else, for free to you, one financial skill.

-Journal how giving makes you feel and notice that shift in perspective.

Mic-Drop Lesson

Tithing is bigger than money. It's time, talent, and treasure. When you give, you don't simply build wealth for yourself; you multiply it in others. That's legacy.

Chapter 14
Your First Financial Binder

The Real Talk

We all have a goal, to maintain our financial lives in our heads: passwords, bills, accounts, balances, and due dates. The result? Missed payments, confusion, and ceaseless stress.

Here's the thing: If your money exists only in your head, you don't really control it. You chase it. That's why there's a financial binder (either physical or digital), and it is one of the smartest moves you can make. It's not just organization; it's empowerment.

Foundation Reminder: What gets documented is what gets managed.

What Is a Financial Binder?

The financial binder is your very own money playbook, all in one spot. If you were to suddenly disappear, a loved one could open your binder and instantly know where things stand.

It includes:

- Bank accounts & logins.
- Budgets (planned vs. actual).
- Debt payoff plans.
- Insurance policies.
- Savings goals.
- Investment accounts.

• Emergency contacts.

• Legacy documents (wills, trusts, beneficiaries). Think of it as your financial GPS. It keeps you from wandering.

Why It Matters

• Clarity: You focus on the entire picture, not pieces of it.

• Accountability: You track progress on goals.

• Preparedness: When something happens to you, loved ones are not left scrambling.

• Confidence: You no longer have to wonder what you need to believe.

Translation: Organization is a moneymaker.

How to Build Your Binder

Choose Your Format

◦ Tangible Connection: A strong folder with tabs, stored securely.

◦ Digital: A secure Excel or password-protected file.

◦ Hybrid: Digital for keeping track, but physical for documents.

Create Sections

◦ Income & Budget → What I thought I'd spend vs. what I spent.

◦ Checking & Savings → Account info, balances, goals.

◦ Debt Tracker → Balances, interest rates, plan.

◦ Insurance → Health, auto, home, life.

◦ Emergency Fund → How Much ("Current balance and what you're adding every month") allocated to the emergency fund account.

◦ Investments → Retirement accounts, stocks, bonds.

◦ Legacy → Wills, beneficiaries, documents.

Update Regularly

◦ Monthly: Budget and account balances.

◦ Quarterly: Debt progress & savings expansion.

◦ Once a Year: Insurance, beneficiaries, long-term goals.

Lesson: A binder is only strong if it's alive, not forgotten.

The Numbers in Real Life

- Binder-less: You have to ask, "How much debt?"

- Using a binder: You can respond in seconds, saying to yourself, "I have $12,300 of debt across 3 accounts with payments totaling $450 each month, bringing it down, and I should be paid off by June 2026." Knowledge brings peace.

Case Study: The Organized Shift

Leah always felt behind financially. At 35, she compiled her first binder, seeing her complete picture: income, debt, savings, and goals. She discovered that it was not altogether how to direct her money; she formulated a real plan and became aggressive about it. One year later, she has gained control over her expenses; she uses a calculated method before making purchases and plans to travel before settling down in her own home.

Lesson: Clarity is the path to confidence.

Faith Connection ◈ Habakkuk 2:2: "Write the vision and make it plain on tablets, that he may run who reads it." Your binder is just you, your vision made plain. It makes sure you are running the right way.

Action Steps for This Chapter

-Choose your binder: physical, digital, or a combination of both.

-Budget, accounts, debt, savings, and legacy would be a good minimum of sections.

-Enter your current numbers, no matter how messy they may be.

-Block 30 minutes on your calendar every month to tweak.

-Inform one single family member other than parents (location + instructions).

Mic-Drop Lesson

A financial binder isn't time-consuming busywork; it's your plan to freedom. Scattered numbers are converted into a story, and that story is a map guiding you from surviving to thriving.

Chapter 15
The Shift

The Real Talk

"Money fear is real. It's your stomach dropping before opening your bank account. It's that fear when you hand the cashier at the grocery store your debit or credit card and then hold your breath, praying the purchase is approved. That fear of the echoing words, "I'm sorry, do you have a different card?" It's the economic panic when a sudden new bill appears. It is the shame of feeling you "should have it together by now." However, the fact is that fear does not derive from money itself. It comes from the unknown. "You don't have any control when you don't know where your money's going.

Foundational Reminder: Clarity meets confidence.

-From Fear to Clarity

• Fear: "I don't know what I owe."

• Clarity: You've written down your debts and come up with a payoff plan.

• Fear: "I can't save."

• Clarity: You've automated $25 into savings each month.

• Fear: "What if something goes wrong?"

• Clarity: You've created a rainy-day fund as your sword.

Lesson: Numbers bring peace.

From Chaos to Control

Chaos is money in all directions and no plan.

-Control is telling your money where to go.

- Budgeting with an actual column.
- Monitoring as your control center.
- Savings as your shield.
- Binder as your road-map. Chaos says, "I hope." Control says, "I know."

-Why This Shift Matters

- It keeps you trapped in survival mode.
- Chaos forces you to be reactive instead of proactive.
- Clarity and control let you breathe, plan, and grow.

Translation: You don't have to make six figures to feel secure. You need a system.

Lesson: Change is internal before it's external.

Faith Connection ◈ Isaiah 41:10: "So do not fear, for I am with you; do not be dismayed, for I am your God. I will uphold you with my right hand of righteousness. God has not called us to live in fear; certainly not in faith, and not even in finances!

-Action Steps for This Chapter

List your 3 most powerful money fears.

Write down one thing that clarifies here for every single challenge.

◦ Fear: "I'll never save." → Step: Open a savings account and transfer $25.

◦ Fear: "My debts I do not know." → Step: Record balances today.

Schedule a monthly "Money Date" with yourself to check in on your budget and binder.

Celebrate any win, no matter how small.

Mic-Drop Lesson

Fear and chaos don't exist when you make more. They depart when you seize control. The change starts with a single choice: I will not be afraid of my money. I will master it."

Epilogue: From Surviving to Stable

Looking Back

"You've walked through the foundation:

• How to budget with honesty, not guilt.

• How to master checking and savings as tools.

• How to protect yourself from overdrafts, debt, and traps.

• How to build emergency funds and positive equity.

• How to tithe not just money but your time and talents.

• How to document your money story in a binder that gives you clarity and control. This wasn't just about numbers. It was about creating peace.

Epilogue Reminder: Stability doesn't come from income; it comes from intention.

What Stability Feels Like

• Bills are paid on time.

• Emergencies don't derail your life.

• You know your debt payoff plan.

• You can breathe when you check your bank account.

• You no longer fear money; you direct it. Translation: You're no longer surviving. You're stable.

Why This Step Matters

Before you can grow wealth, you must protect it. Before you multiply money, you must manage it.

Book 1 gave you the foundation: the steady ground beneath your feet. Without stability, growth feels like gambling. With stability, growth becomes strategy.

The Transition Forward

This is not the end of your journey. It's the launchpad.

Book 2 takes you into growth and multiplication:

- Stocks, bonds, and retirement tools.
- Real estate and land.
- Side hustles and digital assets.
- Multiple streams of income.
- Teaching growth to the next generation.

◈ Luke 16:11: "If you have not been trustworthy in handling worldly wealth, who will trust you with true riches?" You've now built trust with your money. It's time to multiply.

Action for the Next Season

1. Review your financial binder monthly.
2. Strengthen your emergency fund until it feels like a shield.
3. Practice gratitude; stability is wealth in itself.
4. Share what you've learned with another woman.
5. Get ready for Book 2 because now you're ready to grow.

Mic-Drop Lesson

Survival was yesterday. Stability is today. Growth is tomorrow. And legacy is forever."

Acknowledgment of Creative Collaboration

In the development of this book, ChatGPT (OpenAI) was used as a creative partner to assist with brainstorming, clarity, and thematic refinement.

All narratives, perspectives, and core teachings remain the original work of the author.

The technology served only as a support to the writing process, not a substitute for authorship, experience, or voice.

About the Author

Shirley Stephens is a seasoned automotive industry veteran with over 35 years of hands-on experience driving success across dealerships, accounting departments, and training programs. Throughout her career, Shirley has led diverse teams and mentored countless professionals, earning a well-deserved reputation as a powerhouse of knowledge and empowerment.

Armed with dual master's degrees in Integrated Marketing and Marketing, Shirley expertly bridges the gap between deep industry insight and cutting-edge marketing strategies. This unique blend enables her to communicate complex car-buying concepts in a way that's clear, approachable, and actionable for everyday buyers.

What truly sets Shirley apart is her passion for education and empowerment. She understands that buying your first car can feel overwhelming and intimidating, and she's dedicated herself to changing that. Her mission is simple yet powerful: to guide first-time buyers in purchasing the right vehicle, at the right price, and at the right time, all while minimizing stress and maximizing confidence.

Whether she's coaching a first-time car buyer or writing this guide, Shirley's goal remains the same: to equip first-time car buyers with the tools and knowledge to take control of their car-buying journey and make decisions that truly serve their needs and budgets.

When Shirley isn't immersed in the world of cars and marketing, she enjoys reading, gardening, and discovering the next project, which fuels her creativity and keeps her energized for every new challenge.

Don't miss out!

Visit the website below and you can sign up to receive emails whenever SHIRLEY STEPHENS publishes a new book. There's no charge and no obligation.

https://books2read.com/r/B-A-YHRXD-CXAYG

BOOKS 2 READ

Connecting independent readers to independent writers.

Did you love *Own Your Money: The Financial Foundation*? Then you should read *The War Manual: Tactical Prayer Strategies For Women*[1] by SHIRLEY STEPHENS!

[2]

The War Manual: Tactical Prayer Strategies for Women

Life does not hand out battles sparingly; it delivers them daily. Some arrive quietly, as the nagging voice of doubt that whispers you're not enough. Others come roaring, like a storm of disappointment, financial pressure, family conflict, or unexpected loss.

In every case, the outcome depends on how prepared you are to fight.

The War Manual was born out of one simple revelation: God is deliberate and methodical in His instructions for war. Throughout Scripture, battles are never random. They are strategic. God equips His people with clear guidance, weapons of faith, and a mindset for victory.

1. https://books2read.com/u/3nzWpK

2. https://books2read.com/u/3nzWpK

Author Shirley Stephens, a seasoned leader with over 35 years of experience mentoring and empowering others, recognized that the same discipline and strategy that drives success in business and life is also written into the Bible. What began as her personal search for clarity became a resource designed to help others step onto their battlefield with courage and confidence.

Unlike traditional devotionals, The War Manual organizes scripture into a battle plan format. Instead of flipping through the Bible when you're overwhelmed only to feel more lost than when you started, you'll find scriptures arranged topically, giving you direct access to God's Word for the exact challenge you're facing. Whether you are wrestling with fear, fighting discouragement, protecting your family, or standing strong in your purpose, you'll find a clear "war plan" ready to guide you.

Inside, you will discover:

Scriptures framed as strategies for everyday battles of the mind, heart, and spirit.**Practical applications** showing how to use the Word as a weapon in real-life situations.**Topical sections** that address anxiety, temptation, anger, doubt, purpose, and perseverance.**Divine tactics** such as prayer, fasting, praise, and agreement as offensive weapons against life's struggles.**Quick reference guides** so you can immediately find the verses you need in moments of urgency.

This book is not written for the theologian or scholar; it's a written compilation for the everyday believer who sometimes feels worn out, confused, or ill-equipped. It's written for the person who loves God but needs a simple, powerful way to apply His Word when life gets hard. It's written for anyone who has ever thought: If only the Bible came with instructions for today's battles.

With warmth, clarity, and boldness, Shirley Stephens shares the scriptures that carried her through seasons of difficulty and triumph. She does not present them as abstract lessons but as tactical weapons. Every verse is positioned as a command, a defense, or a rallying cry, reminding you that you are not fighting alone, but standing in the strength of a God who has already secured the victory.

Whether you read it cover to cover, use it as a daily devotional, or keep it nearby as a quick-reference guide, The War Manual will become your go-to companion in life's battles. It will train your heart and mind to see challenges not as defeats but as opportunities to step into the arena of faith with confidence.

This is more than a book; it is your personal strategy guide for spiritual warfare.

If you are tired of feeling defeated. If you're ready to silence fear, reclaim your joy, and live with unshakable faith. If you're looking for a practical way to apply God's Word to your daily struggles then it's time to pick up The War Manual and step onto the battlefield prepared.

Victory is not only possible, it's promised. This manual will show you how to claim it, one scripture at a time.

Also by SHIRLEY STEPHENS

Building Financial Confidence Series
Own Your Money: The Financial Foundation

The Awakening Series
Please Don't Eat the Script: Waking Up from the Silent Performance

Standalone
Before You Sign Anything
Built on Reputation
The Power Seat
The Blue Print & The Breakdown
The War Manual: Tactical Prayer Strategies For Women

www.ingramcontent.com/pod-product-compliance
Lightning Source LLC
LaVergne TN
LVHW090425210926
848480LV00002B/684